Scary Creatures
of the
RAINFOREST

Written by
Penny Clarke

BOOK HOUSE

Created and designed
by David Salariya

Author:

Penny Clarke is an author and editor
*specialising in information books for children. She has
written books on natural history, rainforests and
volcanoes, as well as others on different periods of
history. She used to live in central London, but thanks
to modern technology she has now realised her dream
of being able to live and work in the countryside.*

Artists:

John Francis
Robert Morton
Carolyn Scrace
Nicholas Hewetson
Terry Riley
Mark Bergin
Shirley Willis
Lizzie Harper

Series Creator:

David Salariya *was born in Dundee,
Scotland. He established The Salariya Book Company
in 1989. He has illustrated a wide range of books and
has created many new series for publishers in the UK
and overseas. He lives in Brighton with his wife,
illustrator Shirley Willis, and their son.*

Editor: Stephen Haynes

Editorial Assistants:
Rob Walker, Tanya Kant

Picture Research:
Mark Bergin, Carolyn Franklin

Photo Credits:

t=top, b=bottom

Tom Brakefield/Verve: 15b, 18, 22, 25
Cadmium: 8, 15t
John Foxx Images: 12
Mountain High Maps/© 1993 Digital
  Wisdom Inc.: 6–7
Photodisc: 4
PhotoSpin Inc.: 11

Visit our website at **www.book-house.co.uk**
for *free* electronic versions of:
You Wouldn't Want to be an Egyptian Mummy!
You Wouldn't Want to be a Roman Gladiator!
Avoid Joining Shackleton's Polar Expedition!
Avoid Sailing on a 19th-Century Whaling Ship!

Red
piranha

Published in Great Britain in 2008 by
Book House, an imprint of
The Salariya Book Company Ltd
25 Marlborough Place, Brighton BN1 1UB

SALARIYA

A catalogue record for this book is available
from the British Library.

HB ISBN: 978-1-905638-93-2
PB ISBN: 978-1-905638-94-9

Printed in China

PAPER FROM

SUSTAINABLE
FORESTS

Contents

Goliath beetle

What is a rainforest?

This book is about **tropical** rainforests. Forests grow all over the world, but different types of plants grow in different conditions and climates. Tropical rainforests need at least 200 cm of rain that falls evenly throughout the year, and an almost constant temperature of 26°C. Only tropical regions of the world have these conditions.

Tropical rainforests are richer in plants and animals than anywhere else on Earth. Most rainforest trees are very tall, growing to about 50 metres, but a few reach 60 metres. These huge trees provide different **habitats** for the thousands of species living in rainforests.

Emerald tree boa

Emerald tree boas kill by wrapping themselves around their **prey** to crush it.

Emerald tree boa

Heliconid butterfly

Red-eyed tree frog

Topaz hummingbird

Poison-arrow frog

Leaf-cutter ant

Where are the rainforests?

You'll find tropical rainforests in South and Central America, Africa and South-East Asia. They always grow in tropical lowlands, because only there is the climate right for them.

Anacondas are snakes that crush their prey.

Anaconda

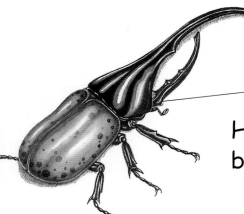

Hercules beetle

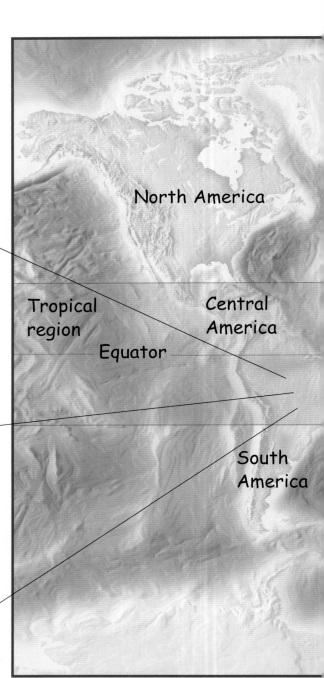

North America

Tropical region

Central America

Equator

South America

Common caiman

Caimans live in the rivers of the Amazon rainforest.

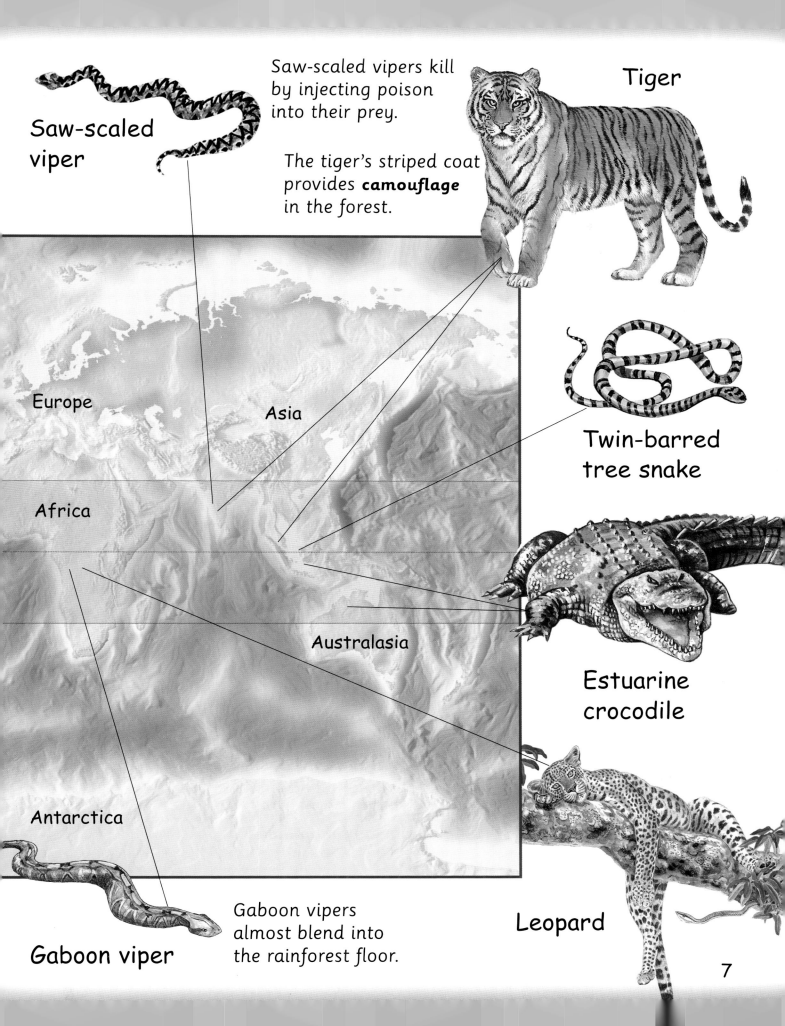

Saw-scaled viper

Saw-scaled vipers kill by injecting poison into their prey.

Tiger

The tiger's striped coat provides **camouflage** in the forest.

Europe

Asia

Africa

Twin-barred tree snake

Australasia

Estuarine crocodile

Antarctica

Gaboon viper

Gaboon vipers almost blend into the rainforest floor.

Leopard

7

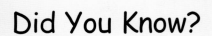
What is interdependence?

Every habitat is the home of many different species. Take away one species, and some others would not survive, because each one depends on several others. This is called 'interdependence'. Rainforest trees provide homes for hundreds of animals, but the trees depend on the animals, too.

Why do plants need animals?

Plants need insects to **pollinate** their flowers. They need birds and other animals to spread their seeds by eating their fruit.

Scientists estimate that every hectare of tropical rainforest has about 750 species of tree, 1,500 other species of plant and 42,000 species of insect – and that's not counting all the birds, reptiles, amphibians and **mammals**!

Pitcher plant

Pitcher plants trap insects in their 'pitchers'.

Keel-billed toucan

Cotton-topped
tamarin

Red-
faced
uakari

Saw-billed hermit
hummingbird

Woolly
monkey

Pierid
butterfly

9

Did You Know?

Scientists divide rainforests into five layers. From the top down, these are: **emergent layer** (the tops of the very tallest trees), **canopy** (the tops of most trees), **understorey** (short, young trees), **shrub layer** (bushes) and **forest floor**.

Are rainforests dark and scary?

It depends where you are. Rainforest trees are so tall and have such thick, leafy tops that little light reaches the ground. So at ground level it is quite dark, but in the treetops it is light.

Bird-eating spiders look much more scary than they really are. They feed on insects, young birds, lizards and frogs.

Meeting a jaguar in the rainforest would be very scary!

Bird-eating spider

What lives in the canopy?

Because the canopy is light and sunny, more creatures live there than anywhere else in the rainforest. Brilliantly coloured birds and butterflies dart about in the canopy, feeding on the bright flowers and fruit.

X-Ray Vision

Hold the next page up to the light to see some of the creatures that live in the rainforest canopy.

See what's inside

Birds' beaks tell you what they eat. Hummingbirds have long, thin beaks to reach nectar deep inside flowers. Macaws (right) crack open nuts with their small, tough beaks. Toucans (below) use their long, curved beaks to pick fruit.

Toucan

Toucans also grab eggs from other birds' nests with their big beaks.

Macaw

The trees of the canopy are not the tallest in the forest. A few even taller ones soar above them. These are the 'forest giants' of the emergent layer, so called because they emerge from the rest of the rainforest.

Macaw

Harpy eagle

Hummingbird

Morpho butterfly

Howler monkey

Squirrel monkey

Three-toed
sloth

Do monkeys live in the rainforest?

Yes! Wherever there are rainforests, there are monkeys. The calls of the howler monkey echo across the forest. Squirrel monkeys scamper through the canopy and into the emergent layer, where danger may lurk as a harpy eagle flies overhead. But the greatest threat is loss of habitat as rainforests are felled.

Squirrel monkey

Squirrel monkeys live in the South American rainforest. They use their long tails to help them balance as they climb and jump through the trees searching for fruit, nuts, insects and birds' nests to raid.

Female orang-utan with baby

Orang-utans live only in the rainforests of South-East Asia. They can use their powerful arms to swing through the trees, but they usually walk along branches (and on the ground) on all fours or upright.

Oasis hummingbird

Glass-wing butterfly

Postman butterfly

Tamandua with its young

Coati

Nine-banded armadillo

16

Up or down?

Even though scientists divide the rainforest into layers, many animals travel from one layer to another. For example, the tamandua or tree anteater lives mainly above the forest floor feeding on ants, but it comes down to the ground if it discovers a termite nest.

Did You Know?

About 50 different species of ant live in the South American rainforest alone. Ants are very good climbers.

Most birds and butterflies live near the canopy, where it is warmest and lightest. But when a giant forest tree comes crashing down, light floods into the lower levels and butterflies and birds start living there – until the trees grow and shut out the light again.

Larger mammals live mainly on the forest floor, although some, like leopards and jaguars, are good climbers. The ground-living South American coati forages in packs of about forty for insects, spiders, lizards and fruit.

Goliath beetle

African goliath beetles are about 10 cm long. Adults live in the canopy, but females fly down to lower levels to lay their eggs.

Can worms really live up in the air?

Yes, they can! Scientists have found worms in crevices of tree trunks many metres above the forest floor. They feed on leaves that fall into the crevices, turning them into compost – just as they would if they lived on the ground. Perhaps their eggs were carried on the feet of ants climbing up and down the tree trunks.

Did You Know?
Some rainforest frogs defend themselves by **secreting** poison through their skins. It is strong enough to kill humans.

Red-eyed tree frog

The red-eyed tree frog is not poisonous. The pike-headed vine snake eats lizards and young birds.

Pike-headed vine snake

Many plants on rainforest trees are **epiphytes**, which means that they grow on the trees but do not harm them. Because these plants contain the green pigment chlorophyll, they can make their own food from sunlight and rain.

Bromeliads are common rainforest plants. You may not have visited a rainforest, but you may have eaten a bromeliad. That cluster of sharp leaves is the clue. The answer? Pineapples are bromeliads!

Water forms pools at the base of bromeliad leaves. Tree frogs lay their eggs in these pools.

Bromeliad

Dragonfly

Skeleton butterfly

19

What happens on the forest floor?

Many creatures living on rainforest floors are small, but without them there would be no rainforest trees and so no rainforests. Why? Because these creatures help provide **nutrients** for the rainforest's trees.

Animals on the forest floor provide the nutrients trees need to survive. These animals break down dead things and release their nutrients into the soil, where tree roots can absorb them.

Did You Know?

In habitats all over the world, dung beetles carry out the essential task of clearing up animal dung.

Crescent-horned dung beetle

Male Hercules beetles can grow up to 17 cm long, but the beakless females are only 9 cm. They lay their eggs in fallen rainforest trees and their tunnelling helps break down the trees.

Hercules beetle

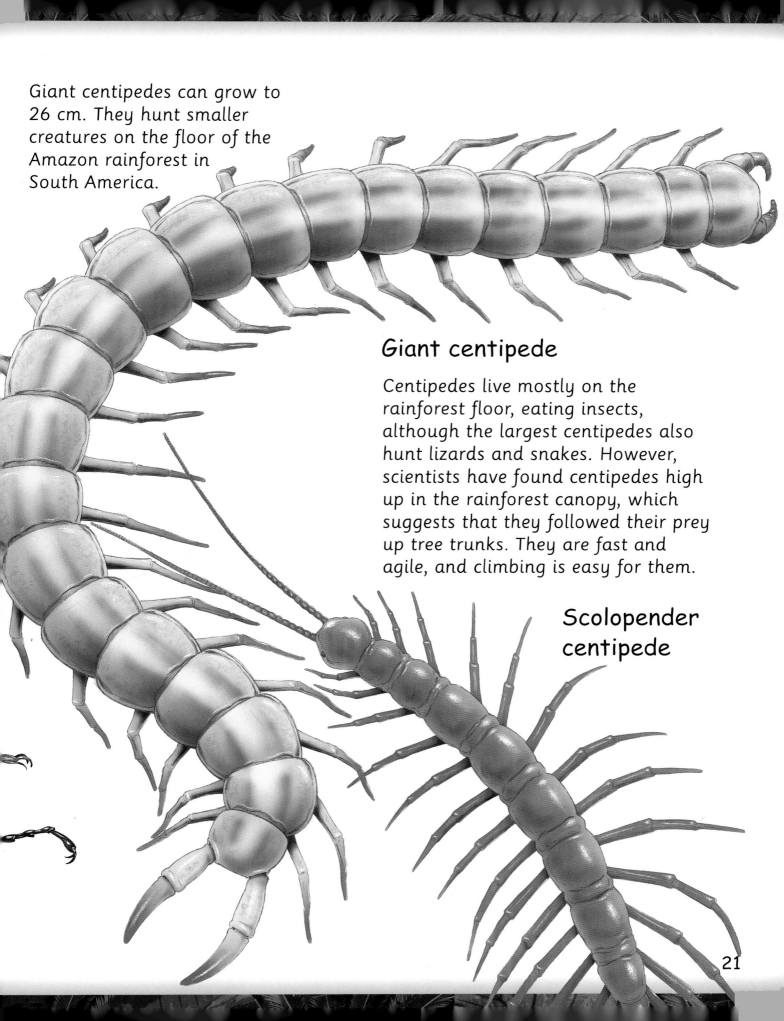

Giant centipedes can grow to 26 cm. They hunt smaller creatures on the floor of the Amazon rainforest in South America.

Giant centipede

Centipedes live mostly on the rainforest floor, eating insects, although the largest centipedes also hunt lizards and snakes. However, scientists have found centipedes high up in the rainforest canopy, which suggests that they followed their prey up tree trunks. They are fast and agile, and climbing is easy for them.

Scolopender centipede

Are there scary creatures in the rainforest?

Yes, every habitat has scary creatures, because every habitat has fierce hunters and other dangerous animals. Not all these creatures are dangerous to humans, though: big cats like leopards and jaguars only attack if they feel threatened.

X-Ray Vision

Hold the next page up to the light to see more scary rainforest creatures.

See what's inside

Strawberry poison-arrow frog

This tiny frog won't attack you, but it is still dangerous. In self-defence it secretes a strong poison. Native peoples of the South American rainforest use the poison on their weapons.

The leopard's spotted coat is good camouflage as it stalks its prey, or waits on a tree branch before dropping onto an antelope passing below.

Leopard

Black leopard
(black panther)

Crocodile

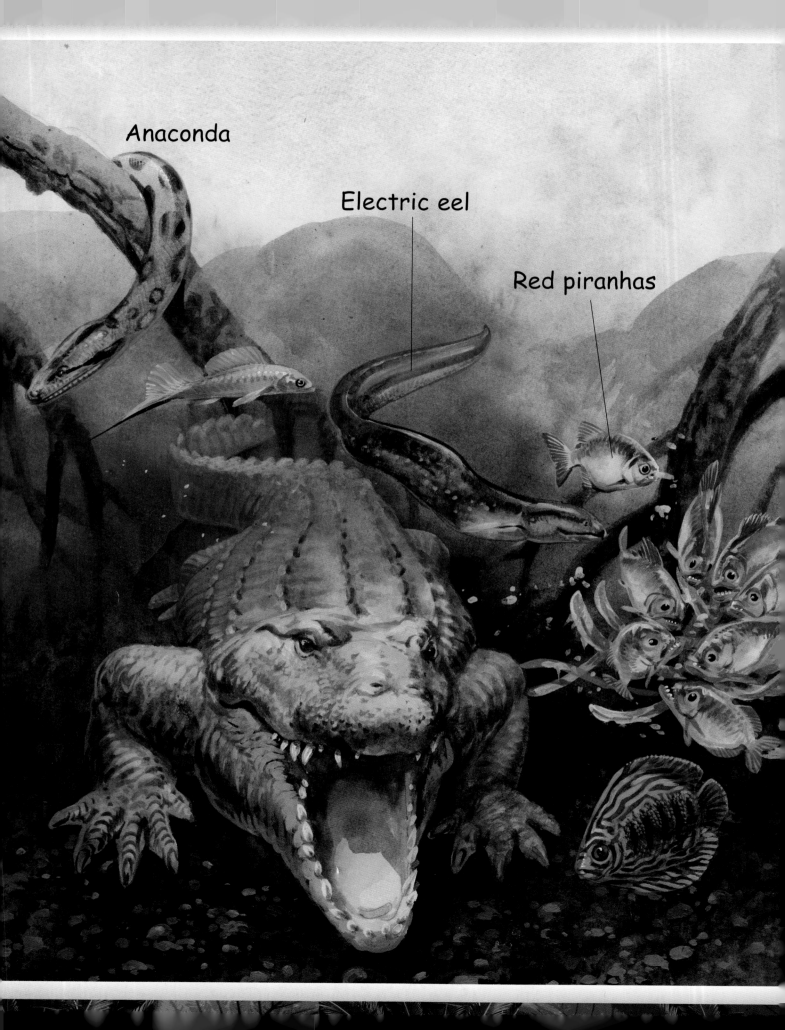

Anaconda

Electric eel

Red piranhas

Nostril

Trachea

Oesophagus

Ribs

Black caiman
(cutaway view)

What lurks in the river?

Huge rivers, like the Amazon in South America and the Congo in Africa, flow through the rainforests. Sunlight floods in and their banks are thick with vegetation. Many unique creatures live in the rivers and along the banks.

'Kill or be killed' applies everywhere in the rainforest, including the rivers. Among the **predators** are members of the crocodile family, the black caiman of the Amazon and the estuarine crocodile of South-East Asia.

Electric eels stun their prey with an electric current. Anacondas lurk on the riverbank, waiting to kill animals coming to drink. But killers don't always win. A shoal of red piranhas (opposite) is eating what the crocodile has just killed.

Crocodile

Poison-tipped arrow

Yanomami village

Yanomami hunter

In the Amazon rainforest the Yanomami people built communal houses called 'malocas'. Every few years they would move on and build another.

Did You Know?

Hunters of both the Yanomami and Matis peoples used to use blowpipes several metres long. They made the pipes from the hollowed-out stems of forest plants. Really skilled hunters could hit a hummingbird's beak.

Matis hunters

Do people live in rainforests?

Rainforests used to be good places for people to live. The forest was so rich in fruits, seeds and nuts that there was no need to grow crops. People just collected what they needed. The men hunted using blowpipes with darts, or bows and arrows. They dipped the tips of their darts or arrows in poison from poison-arrow frogs. But as the rain forest has disappeared, so has this way of life. Few people live in this way today.

Are rainforests in danger?

Sadly, the answer is 'Yes'. All rainforests and the living things they support are in danger. Many countries with rainforests are poor. Some people there think of rainforests as wasted space because crops aren't being grown.

Searching for oil destroys rainforests, but brings companies millions of dollars.

Using their renewable resources, such as latex (rubber), could help rainforests to survive.

Endangered tiger

Rainforest peoples used to make medicines from the forest plants. Destroying the forests and their peoples destroys this knowledge. Fortunately, knowledge of the rosy periwinkle from Madagascar was not lost – it is now used in some cancer treatments.

Shaman making medicine

Quetzal

Did You Know?

Scientists have worked out that rainforest trees release 20 billion tonnes of water into the Earth's atmosphere every day. With no rainforests to do this, there would be much less rainfall around the world.

Rainforest facts

Malaria, a disease which can kill humans, is spread by mosquitoes. Quinine, the first treatment for malaria, was made from the bark of the cinchona tree from the South American rainforest.

Rubber is made from the sap of a tree that first grew in the Amazon rainforest.

All mammals breathe in oxygen and breathe out carbon dioxide. Trees and plants, on the other hand, absorb carbon dioxide. Cutting down rainforests will mean that less carbon dioxide can be absorbed. Scientists think that too much carbon dioxide in the atmosphere will increase global warming.

Birds of paradise live only in the Asian rainforests. The forests are so dense that no-one is sure how many species there are.

The three-toed sloth moves very, very slowly. It has special grooved hairs in its coat in which green algae grow. They help camouflage the sloth by making it look like the leafy branches among which it lives.

Once an area of rainforest has been cut down, it can never grow again. There is no more vegetation to protect the thin soil, which is soon washed or blown away.

Many rainforest trees have two sorts of roots: ordinary roots and buttress roots. Buttress roots grow down the outside of a tree's trunk and into the ground. Without these, the tree would not be able to support itself in the shallow rainforest soil.

If you want to help the rainforests, you can support environmental organisations and learn as much as you can about the rainforest and its wildlife. Take care not to buy anything that might have come from a rainforest. This could be a bird or some other animal (jewellery made from butterflies' wings has been fashionable in the past), or something made from rainforest wood. And always ignore anyone who tells you that one person's action won't make any difference.

Glossary

camouflage Any special markings or colouring on an animal that help it to blend in with its surroundings.

canopy The layer of the rainforest where the tops of most of the trees are.

emergent layer The tops of the tallest trees in the rainforest.

endangered In danger of dying out.

epiphyte Any plant that grows on other plants (mostly trees) without harming them. Epiphytes get water from rain trapped in their leaves, not through their roots.

forest floor The lowest level of the rainforest.

habitat The place where a particular type of plant or animal lives naturally.

mammal A hairy or furry animal that feeds on its mother's milk when it is young.

nutrient Any substance that gives nourishment.

pollinate To exchange pollen between flowering plants. If its flowers are not pollinated, a plant cannot produce its fruit or seeds.

predator Any animal that hunts other animals for food.

prey Any creature that is hunted for food by other animals.

secrete To produce or give off a substance.

shaman A wise man or healer in a native tribe.

shrub layer The second-lowest level of the forest, where shrubs and small trees grow.

species A group of plants or animals that look alike, live in the same way and produce young that do the same.

White-tailed deer

tropical Belonging to the tropics – the region of the Earth that is between the Tropic of Cancer north of the Equator and the Tropic of Capricorn south of the Equator. This area has the warmest climate on Earth.

understorey The level of the rainforest where the younger and shorter trees are.

Index